I0821237

New York METS

KENNY ABDO

Fly!
An Imprint of Abdo Zoom
abdobooks.com

abdobooks.com

Published by Abdo Zoom, a division of ABDO, P.O. Box 398166, Minneapolis, Minnesota 55439.

Printed in the United States of America, North Mankato, Minnesota.
102025
012026

Photo Credits: AP Images, Getty Images, Shutterstock
Production Contributors: Kenny Abdo, Jennie Forsberg, Grace Hansen
Design Contributors: Candice Keimig, Neil Klinepier

Library of Congress Control Number: 2025936767

Publisher's Cataloging-in-Publication Data

Names: Abdo, Kenny, author.
Title: New York Mets / by Kenny Abdo
Description: Minneapolis, Minnesota : Abdo Zoom, 2026 | Series: MLB teams | Includes online resources and index.
Identifiers: ISBN 9798384940265 (lib. bdg.) | ISBN 9798384941026 (ebook) | ISBN 9798384941408 (read-to-me ebook)
Subjects: LCSH: New York Mets (Baseball team)--Juvenile literature. | Baseball teams--Juvenile literature. | Professional sports--Juvenile literature. | Sports franchises--Juvenile literature. | Major League Baseball (Organization)--Juvenile literature.
Classification: DDC 796.357--dc23

Table of CONTENTS

METS

With the hustle of Times Square and ups and downs like the city skyline, the New York Mets are a perfect slice of the Big Apple!

With a deep bench of all-time greats, the Mets have delivered thrilling wins and tough losses, giving the City That Never Sleeps a good reason to stay wide awake!

IGLESIAS
11
6
24
24

BATTER UP!

The New York Mets played their first season in 1962. The team was created to bring **National League** (**NL**) baseball back to New York. Its colors honored the former New York Giants and Brooklyn Dodgers.

The Mets got off to a rough start, losing a record-setting 120 games and finishing last in their first season.

Rising star Richie Ashburn hit .306 and made the **All-Star** team in his only year with the Mets.

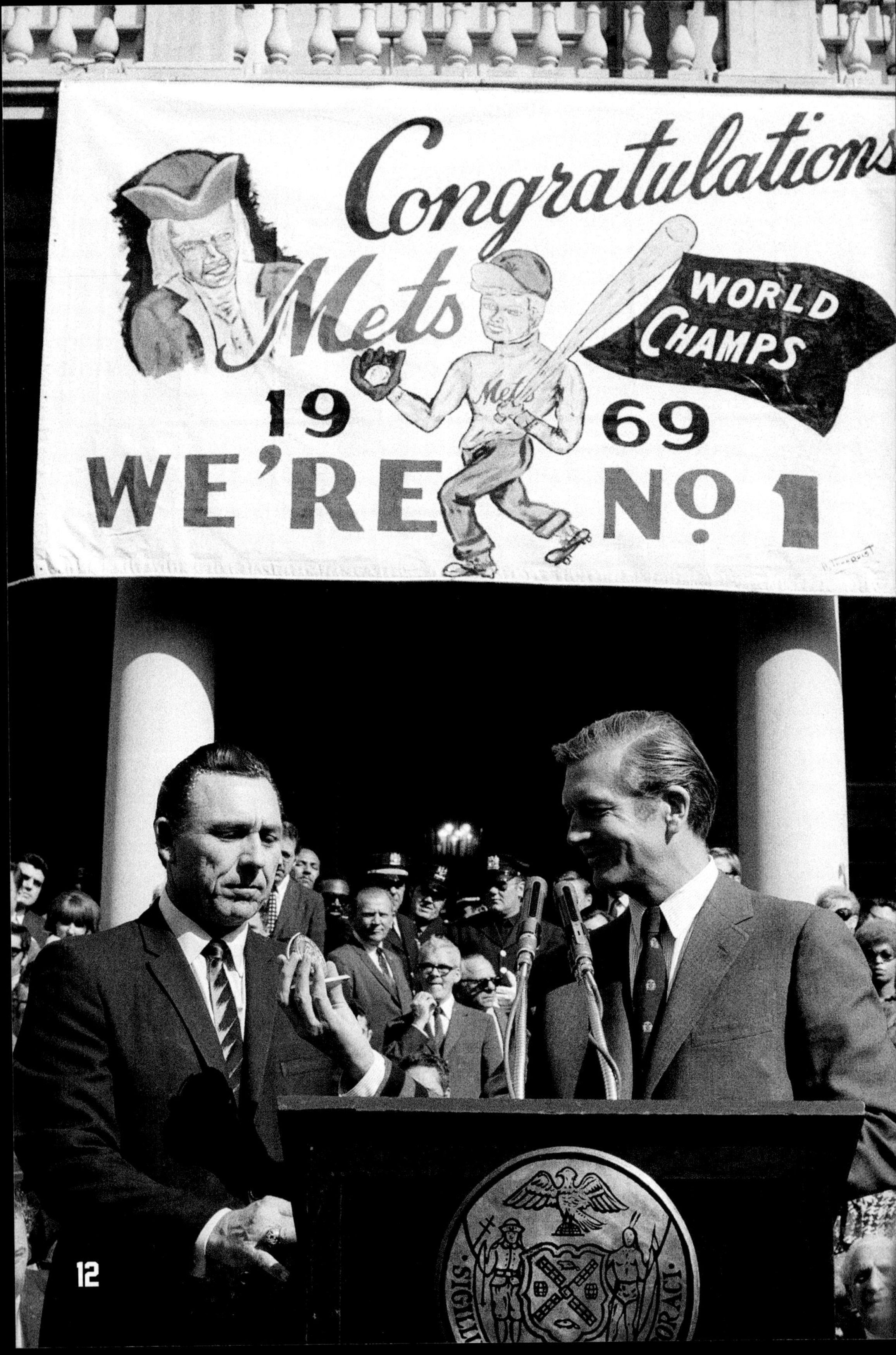

Congratulations
Mets
WORLD CHAMPS
1969
WE'RE No 1

In 1969, the "Miracle Mets" shocked the baseball world. The team won the World Series by defeating the Orioles in five games! It was one of the biggest **upsets** in baseball history.

GRAND SLAMS

In 1973, Tom Seaver met rivals with blazing fast pitches and a 2.08 **ERA**. The Mets won the **NL pennant** and reached the World Series. They lost to the Athletics in seven games. That season, the team's rallying cry was, "You Gotta Believe!"

The Mets struggled for years, but as 1986 opened, the Mets looked unbeatable. They finished the season winning 108 games, a team **record**. The playoffs were not easy, but the Mets moved on to play the Red Sox in the World Series. Spurred by an incredible three-run comeback in the 10th inning of Game 6, the Mets won it all in Game 7!

MIKE
86

NY
Mets
34

Mike Piazza helped the Mets reach the World Series again in 2000. The team faced the Yankees but lost in five games. In 2015, with strong pitching from Jacob deGrom and Noah Syndergaard, the Mets won the **NL pennant** and returned to the World Series. However, they fell to the Royals.

The Mets added rising stars like first baseman Pete Alonso in 2019 and shortstop Francisco Lindor in 2021. In 2022, the Mets won 101 games and returned to the playoffs as a **wild-card** team.

NY

The 2023 and 2024 seasons came with ups and downs, including major injuries and roster changes. Early in the 2025 season, the Mets seemed unstoppable in both hitting and pitching. They went on to have a late-season slump. Fans still hope that the team's next championship is just around the corner.

NewYork-Presbyterian
20

HALL OF FAME

Tom Seaver won 198 games and struck out 2,541 batters with the Mets. He led the team to its first World Series title in 1969. Seaver earned all three of his **Cy Young Awards** while in New York. In 1992, he became the first Mets player named to the Baseball Hall of Fame.

AWARD
CY YOUNG AWARD
Mets

Darryl Strawberry hit 252 home runs with the Mets and made seven straight **All-Star** teams. He helped the team win the 1986 World Series and led the Mets in home runs for seven seasons in a row!

Mets
18

Rawlings
Rawlings
Rawlings

Mike Piazza hit 220 home runs as a Met and became one of the best-hitting catchers in baseball history. In 1999, he smashed 40 home runs, setting a Mets **record** for a catcher. Piazza helped lead the team to the World Series in 2000 and made six **All-Star** teams. He was **inducted** into the Baseball Hall of Fame in 2016.

GLOSSARY

All-Star – consisting of athletes chosen as the best at their positions from all teams in a league or region.

Cy Young Award – an annual American baseball award given to the best pitcher in each of the two MLB leagues.

Earned-Run Average (ERA) – the average number of earned runs per game scored against a pitcher.

inducted – brought in as a member.

National League (NL) – one of two 15-team leagues that make up MLB.

pennant – the title achieved by the team that wins its division or league championship.

record – a top achievement by a team or player that no one has done before.

upset – a victory by a team that was not expected to win.

wild-card – a place or a team chosen to fill a place in a competition after the regularly qualified players or teams have all been decided.

ONLINE RESOURCES

To learn more about the New York Mets, please visit **abdobooklinks.com** or scan this QR code. These links are routinely monitored and updated to provide the most current information available.

INDEX